Jossey-Bass Teacher

Jossey-Bass Teacher provides K–12 teachers with essential knowledge and tools to create a positive and lifelong impact on student learning. Trusted and experienced educational mentors offer practical classroom-tested and theory-based teaching resources for improving teaching practice in a broad range of grade levels and subject areas. From one educator to another, we want to be your first source to make every day your best day in teaching. *Jossey-Bass Teacher* resources serve two types of informational needs—essential knowledge and essential tools.

Essential knowledge resources provide the foundation, strategies, and methods from which teachers may design curriculum and instruction to challenge and excite their students. Connecting theory to practice, essential knowledge books rely on a solid research base and time-tested methods, offering the best ideas and guidance from many of the most experienced and well-respected experts in the field.

Essential tools save teachers time and effort by offering proven, ready-to-use materials for in-class use. Our publications include activities, assessments, exercises, instruments, games, ready reference, and more. They enhance an entire course of study, a weekly lesson, or a daily plan. These essential tools provide insightful, practical, and comprehensive materials on topics that matter most to K–12 teachers.

Fantasy Soccer and Mathematics

Student Name: _____

Fantasy Sports and Mathematics Series

Fantasy Soccer and Mathematics

Student Workbook

Dan Flockhart

JOSSEY-BASS

Published by Jossey-Bass
A Wiley Imprint
989 Market Street, San Francisco, CA 94103-1741   www.josseybass.com

ISBN: 0-978-7879-9450-1

Printed in the United States of America
FIRST EDITION
PB Printing   10 9 8 7 6 5 4 3 2 1

About the Author

Dan Flockhart received his multiple-subject teaching credential from California State University, East Bay in 1988. He taught mathematics in grades 5 through 8 for eleven years at St. Matthew's Episcopal Day School in San Mateo, California, where he incorporated fantasy sports into his math curriculum. He has also taught general studies classes at College of the Redwoods in Eureka, California. He received a master of arts degree in education from Humboldt State University in 2005; the title of his thesis was "Teacher Perceptions of the Effects of Fantasy Football in the Teaching of Mathematics." Flockhart has enjoyed participating in fantasy sports for over twenty-five years.

In addition to authoring the Fantasy Sports and Mathematics series, Flockhart maintains a Web site, www.fantasysportsmath.com, where teachers can participate in forums and contests and find out more about the series.

To my girls

Acknowledgments

I am grateful to Tiffany for her love and support, as well as the many hours she spent on this project. I am also thankful to Kate, who made all of this possible. You are one of my angels! I was also lucky to work with wonderful production editors, Elizabeth and Susan, and copyeditors, Carolyn and Bev. They were fun to work with and I was impressed with their willingness to do whatever it took to produce the best possible product. My thanks go out as well to Chris for creating one of the best covers I've ever seen. In addition, I'm grateful to Lena for ensuring that all the math is accurate. Thanks to Annie for being by my side and providing me with the inspiration I needed to finish this project.

Contents

Assessment   143

Fantasy Soccer and Mathematics Handouts

Description and Rules

Fantasy Soccer and Mathematics is a game in which you create and manage a team of professional, college, or high school soccer players. You may select players from one country or combine players from different countries. Players earn points based on their performance in their games. Each week you will use newspapers or online resources to locate your players' statistics. Then you will find the sum of the points your players earned by using a scoring system provided by your teacher. The goal of the game is to accumulate the highest number of points.

How to Select Players

Most soccer teams play one game a week. In the United States, the Major League Soccer season begins in April and concludes in mid-October. In all other countries, the soccer club season begins in July or August and concludes the following May. Players earn points from their performances in their club games, as opposed to games at the international level, which includes regional games, World Cup games, and "friendlies" (exhibition matches between teams from two countries).

You may select players from any country that has a professional league; they can be women players, men players, or a combination of men and women players on a single team. There are 207 countries that have professional soccer leagues for men. Germany, Sweden, France, England, Norway, and Japan have professional leagues for women.

Select eighteen players for your team. Seven players will be substitutes in case a starting player is injured or performs poorly. You may select players at any position (although your teacher may change this rule), with the exception that you must choose a minimum of two goalkeepers. You may select the same players as other students.

Each week you will start eleven players, including one goalkeeper. Each player in a starting lineup should play for a different team, provided that you select players from leagues that contain a minimum of eleven teams. If fewer than eleven teams are available from which to select players, then divide 18 by the number of teams, and round the quotient down to the nearest whole number. For example, if you selected players from a league that had 8 teams, you would divide 18 by 8 to arrive at 2.25, and round the quotient down to 2. Consequently, you would need to select a minimum of two players from each team in the league. In the case of Major League Soccer (the professional league in the United States), there are more than eleven teams, so you would select a minimum of one player from each team.

If you want to choose players who play in the professional league in the United States, you can visit www.fantasysportsmath.com and click on "Get Soccer Stats." On the following page, click on the "Players" link on the left-hand side of the page. This will take you to a list of all players in the league.

Description and Rules *(Cont'd.)*

If you want to select players from countries other than the United States, you can visit www.fantasysportsmath.com and click on "Get Soccer Stats." This will lead to the home page for the Fédération Internationale de Football Association (FIFA). For example, let's say you wanted to pick players from Germany. On the FIFA home page, click on the "Associations FIFA" drop-down menu. (*Note:* It's best to use the Internet Explorer browser if you select players from countries other than the United States.) You will see links to all countries that are members of FIFA. Select Germany. Then click on the link at the top of the page for professional soccer leagues in Germany: http://www.dfb.de. On the following page there is an option to choose an English-translated version of the Web site by clicking on the "English version" link at the top right of the page. The top professional league in Germany is Bundesliga. Click on the Bundesliga link on the top left of the page. This will take you to a page that lists the three professional leagues in Germany: Bundesliga (the top team), 2 Bundesliga, and Women's Bundesliga.

If you want to select women players from Germany, click on the "Women's Bundesliga" link. On the following page, select "Addresses." This link takes you to a page that lists the Web site addresses for all of the teams in the women's professional league. If you want to select players from FFC Frankfurt, click on that team's address (www.ffc-frankfurt.de). On the FFC Frankfurt home page, click on the "Bundesligateam" link on the left side of the page, and the team roster will appear.

If you want to choose men players who play in Germany, select the "Bundeslige" link at the top left of the Bundeslige home page. Then select the first Bundesliga located at the top of the following page. On the following page, select "Addresses." This link takes you to a page that lists the Web site addresses for all of the teams in the league. If you want to select players from Hertha BSC Berlin, click on that team's address (www. herthabsc.de). You will be directed to a page that gives you the opportunity to choose one of four languages. Once you are on the Hertha BSC Berlin home page, click on the "Team" link on the top left of the page, and the team roster will appear.

As another example, suppose you want to select players who play in the professional league in China. Visit www.fantasysportsmath.com and click on "Get Soccer Stats." Select China PR from the Associations FIFA drop-down menu on the FIFA home page. (You should use the Internet Explorer browser if you don't speak Mandarin.) You will be taken to the home page for soccer in China (www.fa.org.cn). Click on the link "China League." (At the time of this writing, the link is located in the middle of the page and is the only text on the page that is written in English.) This takes you to a page that lists the logos for the teams in the league. Click on any team logo, and the team roster will appear.

The process of locating players from different countries varies, but you should be able to locate the top professional players from any country provided that you understand the language on the Web sites you are accessing. Some Web sites provide alternative-language versions, and others do not.

Description and Rules *(Cont'd.)*

Trades

You may trade players with your classmates. However, each week you should be able to field a full starting lineup consisting of eleven players, including one goalkeeper. You cannot select additional players once the game begins. Consequently, it is important to keep as many players as possible on your roster in case of injuries.

Injuries

Lists of injured players from the U.S. professional leagues are printed in major newspapers and can also be accessed through www.fantasysportsmath.com by clicking on "Get Soccer Stats." On the next page, click on "News." On the News page, click on the "View All Injuries" link, located in the "Injuries and Discipline" section.

You can find a list of injuries for players who play in countries other than the United States online or in major newspapers from those countries. If you cannot locate a player's name in the box scores, he or she is probably injured. *If this occurs, the player's score is counted as zero.*

Fantasy Team Roster

Name of Fantasy Team: _____   Team Owner: _____

Player	Team

How to Read Box Scores

Box scores vary in format as well as the information they provide. The fabricated box score provided below for a game between the Fortuna Huskies and Scotia Bears is formatted along the lines of those on the Major League Soccer Web site at www.MLSnet.com. The game stats are provided in Table 1.

Scoring

FORTUNA—Rinalo Ellis 1 (Gary Hope 1) 8
FORTUNA—Carmelo Blase 1 (Brian Moor 1) 21
SCOTIA—Ming Ho 1 (Jorge Sadon 1) 32
FORTUNA—Lars Visser 1 (Rinalo Ellis 1, Gary Hope 2) 54
SCOTIA—Livan Slevin 1 (Ming Ho 1, Jorge Sadon 2) 60
SCOTIA—Pedro Garcia 1 (Livan Slevin 1, Jorge Sadon 3) 83

Discipline

FORTUNA—Rinalo Ellis (caution; Pushing, Holding) 14
FORTUNA—Yi Chen (caution; Tackle from Behind) 45
FORTUNA—Gary Hope (ejection; Serious Foul Play) 60
SCOTIA—Ming Ho (ejection; Serious Foul Play) 61
SCOTIA—Denzel Plates (caution; Professional Foul) 72
SCOTIA—Livan Slevin (caution; Reckless Foul) 88

In the Scoring section above, the first player listed (Ellis) scored the goal. The number after each player's name is the number of goals he scored in the game. The last number in each string represents the minute of the game in which the goal occurred. In this game, no player scored more than one goal.

Table 1. Game Stats for Fortuna Huskies versus Scotia Bears

	Fortuna	Scotia
Total shots	8	11
Shots on goal	5	4
Total saves	4	6
Fouls	12	16
Offsides	3	2
Corner kicks	2	5

How to Read Box Scores *(Cont'd.)*

Players whose names are in parentheses are credited with an assist. If two players are listed in parentheses, those two are both credited with an assist. The number after each name in parentheses represents the number of assists that person accumulated. For example, Jorge Sadon had three assists because his name is listed in parentheses on three different occasions next to the numbers 1, 2, and 3, respectively.

The Discipline section lists players who received cautions (yellow cards) or ejections (red cards), along with explanations for their penalties and the minute of the game in which they occurred.

Table 1 has four sections you will use: total shots (the total number of shots taken by a team in the game), total saves (the number of goals saved by a team), fouls (the number of fouls committed by a team), and offsides (the number of times players on one team were caught offsides). You do not have to understand the technical aspects of the game because the numbers given are straightforward.

A hypothetical starting team is listed in Table 2. All players on this team are fabricated and used extensively for reference purposes throughout this book. All graphs and several worksheets are linked to this team. For simplicity, all players on this team are listed in the Fortuna-Scotia box score. This will not occur when you play because you will select players from several different teams.

Table 2. Starting Lineup for the Panthers

Player	Team
Yi Chen (goalkeeper)	Fortuna
Jorge Sadon	Scotia
Ming Ho	Scotia
Brian Moor	Fortuna
Denzel Plates	Scotia
Pedro Garcia	Scotia
Livan Slevin	Scotia
Gary Hope	Fortuna
Lars Visser	Fortuna
Rinalo Ellis	Fortuna

Fantasy Soccer and Mathematics handouts

How to Collect Data

Each week, you will access box scores online or in newspapers to locate statistics for your players. Most teams play one game a week. In the United States, Major League Soccer's season begins in April and concludes in mid-October. Most games are played on Saturdays, Sundays, and Wednesdays, and a few games are played on Thursdays and Fridays. In other countries, the soccer club season begins in July or August and concludes the following May. Players earn points from performances in their club games, as opposed to games at the international level, which includes regional games, World Cup games, and "friendlies" (exhibition matches between teams from two countries). Players occasionally leave their clubs for a short time to play in international matches or regional competition. If you cannot locate a player's name in box scores, that person may be playing for a national team or may have been injured or suspended. The process of collecting data varies according to the country and the corresponding Web sites and newspapers that contain players' statistics.

If the players on your team are in the professional league in the United States, you can visit www.fantasysportsmath.com, and do the following:

1. Click on "Get Soccer Stats."

2. On the following page, click on the "Scoreboard" link on the left side of the page to highlight the previous week's games. (If you are looking for a different week you can use the drop-down menu at the top of the page. Statistics are archived online, so you can access the data if you missed a week or two.)

3. Once you are on the page that highlights the games from the specified week, you can locate a player's team and click on the "Match Tracker" link below that game. This will take you to the box score for that game.

If you have players on your team who play in professional leagues in countries other than the United States, you can access their statistics by using newspapers from those countries or logging onto that country's Web site, which can be accessed by visiting www.fantasysportsmath.com and clicking on "Get Soccer Stats." Once you are on the FIFA home page, the "Associations FIFA" drop-down menu contains links to all countries that are members of FIFA.

How to Compute Points: Default Scoring System

The default scoring system can be used each week to determine the ranking of students' teams in the game. It was designed so that you can plot the weekly points earned for your players on a variety of graphs. Your teacher may choose a different scoring system that is more appropriate for you.

For Each:		Players Earn:	
Goal (G)		$\frac{1}{4}$	or	.250
Save (S)		$\frac{1}{6}$	or	.167
Assist (A)		$\frac{1}{6}$	or	.167
Caution (yellow card) (Y)		$-\frac{1}{12}$	or	.083
Ejection (red card) (R)		$-\frac{1}{12}$	or	−.083
		Players' Teams Earn:	
Total shots (T)		$\frac{1}{8}$	or	.125
Fouls (F)		$-\frac{1}{24}$	or	−.042
Offsides (O)		$-\frac{1}{24}$	or	−.042

Note: Decimals are rounded to the nearest thousandth.

Practice in Computing Points Using the Default Scoring System

Use the following chart to compute points for the players listed in the Fortuna-Scotia box score in Handout 3.

Player	Number of Goals $\times \frac{1}{4}$	Number of Saves and Assists $\times \frac{1}{6}$	Number of Yellow Cards and Red Cards $\times \left(-\frac{1}{12}\right)$	Number of Total Shots by Player's Team $\times \frac{1}{8}$	Number of Fouls and Offsides by Player's Team $\times \left(-\frac{1}{24}\right)$	Total Points for Player and Player's Team
Chen	0	$\frac{4}{6}$	$-\frac{1}{12}$	$\frac{8}{8}$	$-\frac{15}{24}$	$\frac{23}{24}$
Sadon						
Ho						
Moor						
Plates						
Garcia						
Slevin						
Hope						
Visser						
Ellis						
Blase						
Total team points (the sum of the values in the last column):						

Default Total Points Equation

In this equation, the numerical values are the same as the default scoring system:

$$\frac{1}{4}(G) + \frac{1}{6}(S + A) - \frac{1}{12}(Y + R) + \frac{1}{8}(T) - \frac{1}{24}(F + O) = W$$

G = number of goals scored by player
S = number of saves by player
A = number of assists by player
Y = number of yellow cards (cautions) for player
R = number of red cards (ejection) for player
T = number of total shots by player's team
F = number of fouls by player's team
O = number of offsides by player's team
W = total points earned for one game for one player and the player's team

Practice in Computing Points Using the Default Total Points Equation

Use Handout 3 and the following equation to compute points for the players listed below:

$$\frac{1}{4}(G) + \frac{1}{6}(S + A) - \frac{1}{12}(Y + R) + \frac{1}{8}(T) - \frac{1}{24}(F + O) = W$$

Yi Chen

$$\frac{1}{4}(0) + \frac{1}{6}(4 + 0) - \frac{1}{12}(1 + 0) + \frac{1}{8}(8) - \frac{1}{24}(12 + 3) = \frac{23}{24}$$

Jorge Sadon

Ming Ho

Brian Moor

Denzel Plates

Pedro Garcia

Livan Slevin

Gary Hope

Lars Visser

Rinalo Ellis

Carmelo Blase

Total points for the Panthers: _____

HANDOUT 9

Weekly Scoring Worksheet (Week 1)

Your teacher will help you to fill in the numerical values for scoring criteria in the top row.

Player	Number of Goals × _____	Number of Saves and Assists × _____	Number of Yellow Cards and Red Cards × _____	Number of Total Shots by Player's Team × _____	Number of Fouls and Offsides by Player's Team × _____	Total Points for Player and Player's Team × _____
Total points (the sum of the values in the last column):						

Weekly Scoring Worksheet (Week 2)

Your teacher will help you to fill in the numerical values for scoring criteria in the top row.

Player	Number of Goals × _____	Number of Saves and Assists × _____	Number of Yellow Cards and Red Cards × _____	Number of Total Shots by Player's Team × _____	Number of Fouls and Offsides by Player's Team × _____	Total Points for Player and Player's Team × _____
Total points (the sum of the values in the last column):						

Weekly Scoring Worksheet (Week 3)

Your teacher will help you to fill in the numerical values for scoring criteria in the top row.

Player	Number of Goals × _____	Number of Saves and Assists × _____	Number of Yellow Cards and Red Cards × _____	Number of Total Shots by Player's Team × _____	Number of Fouls and Offsides by Player's Team × _____	Total Points for Player and Player's Team × _____
Total points (the sum of the values in the last column):						

Weekly Scoring Worksheet (Week 4)

Your teacher will help you to fill in the numerical values for scoring criteria in the top row.

Player	Number of Goals × _____	Number of Saves and Assists × _____	Number of Yellow Cards and Red Cards × _____	Number of Total Shots by Player's Team × _____	Number of Fouls and Offsides by Player's Team × _____	Total Points for Player and Player's Team × _____
Total points (the sum of the values in the last column):						

Weekly Scoring Worksheet (Week 5)

Your teacher will help you to fill in the numerical values for scoring criteria in the top row.

Player	Number of Goals × _____	Number of Saves and Assists × _____	Number of Yellow Cards and Red Cards × _____	Number of Total Shots by Player's Team × _____	Number of Fouls and Offsides by Player's Team × _____	Total Points for Player and Player's Team × _____
Total points (the sum of the values in the last column):						

Weekly Scoring Worksheet (Week 6)

Your teacher will help you to fill in the numerical values for scoring criteria in the top row.

Player	Number of Goals × _____	Number of Saves and Assists × _____	Number of Yellow Cards and Red Cards × _____	Number of Total Shots by Player's Team × _____	Number of Fouls and Offsides by Player's Team × _____	Total Points for Player and Player's Team × _____
Total points (the sum of the values in the last column):						

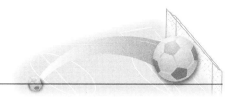

Weekly Scoring Worksheet (Week 7)

Your teacher will help you to fill in the numerical values for scoring criteria in the top row.

Player	Number of Goals × _____	Number of Saves and Assists × _____	Number of Yellow Cards and Red Cards × _____	Number of Total Shots by Player's Team × _____	Number of Fouls and Offsides by Player's Team × _____	Total Points for Player and Player's Team × _____
Total points (the sum of the values in the last column):						

Fantasy Soccer and Mathematics handouts

Weekly Scoring Worksheet (Week 8)

Your teacher will help you to fill in the numerical values for scoring criteria in the top row.

Player	Number of Goals × _____	Number of Saves and Assists × _____	Number of Yellow Cards and Red Cards × _____	Number of Total Shots by Player's Team × _____	Number of Fouls and Offsides by Player's Team × _____	Total Points for Player and Player's Team × _____
Total points (the sum of the values in the last column):						

Weekly Scoring Worksheet (Week 9)

Your teacher will help you to fill in the numerical values for scoring criteria in the top row.

Player	Number of Goals ✕ _____	Number of Saves and Assists ✕ _____	Number of Yellow Cards and Red Cards ✕ _____	Number of Total Shots by Player's Team ✕ _____	Number of Fouls and Offsides by Player's Team ✕ _____	Total Points for Player and Player's Team ✕ _____
Total points (the sum of the values in the last column):						

Fantasy Soccer and Mathematics handouts

Peer Signature: _____

Weekly Scoring Worksheet (Week 10)

Your teacher will help you to fill in the numerical values for scoring criteria in the top row.

Player	Number of Goals × _____	Number of Saves and Assists × _____	Number of Yellow Cards and Red Cards × _____	Number of Total Shots by Player's Team × _____	Number of Fouls and Offsides by Player's Team × _____	Total Points for Player and Player's Team × _____
Total points (the sum of the values in the last column):						

Weekly Scoring Worksheet (Week 11)

Your teacher will help you to fill in the numerical values for scoring criteria in the top row.

Player	Number of Goals × _____	Number of Saves and Assists × _____	Number of Yellow Cards and Red Cards × _____	Number of Total Shots by Player's Team × _____	Number of Fouls and Offsides by Player's Team × _____	Total Points for Player and Player's Team × _____
Total points (the sum of the values in the last column):						

Weekly Scoring Worksheet (Week 12)

Your teacher will help you to fill in the numerical values for scoring criteria in the top row.

Player	Number of Goals ✕ _____	Number of Saves and Assists ✕ _____	Number of Yellow Cards and Red Cards ✕ _____	Number of Total Shots by Player's Team ✕ _____	Number of Fouls and Offsides by Player's Team ✕ _____	Total Points for Player and Player's Team ✕ _____
Total points (the sum of the values in the last column):						

Weekly Scoring Worksheet (Week 13)

Your teacher will help you to fill in the numerical values for scoring criteria in the top row.

Player	Number of Goals ✕ _____	Number of Saves and Assists ✕ _____	Number of Yellow Cards and Red Cards ✕ _____	Number of Total Shots by Player's Team ✕ _____	Number of Fouls and Offsides by Player's Team ✕ _____	Total Points for Player and Player's Team ✕ _____
Total points (the sum of the values in the last column):						

Weekly Scoring Worksheet (Week 14)

Your teacher will help you to fill in the numerical values for scoring criteria in the top row.

Player	Number of Goals × _____	Number of Saves and Assists × _____	Number of Yellow Cards and Red Cards × _____	Number of Total Shots by Player's Team × _____	Number of Fouls and Offsides by Player's Team × _____	Total Points for Player and Player's Team × _____
Total points (the sum of the values in the last column):						

Weekly Scoring Worksheet (Week 15)

Your teacher will help you to fill in the numerical values for scoring criteria in the top row.

Player	Number of Goals × _____	Number of Saves and Assists × _____	Number of Yellow Cards and Red Cards × _____	Number of Total Shots by Player's Team × _____	Number of Fouls and Offsides by Player's Team × _____	Total Points for Player and Player's Team × _____
Total points (the sum of the values in the last column):						

Weekly Scoring Worksheet (Week 16)

Your teacher will help you to fill in the numerical values for scoring criteria in the top row.

Player	Number of Goals × _____	Number of Saves and Assists × _____	Number of Yellow Cards and Red Cards × _____	Number of Total Shots by Player's Team × _____	Number of Fouls and Offsides by Player's Team × _____	Total Points for Player and Player's Team × _____
Total points (the sum of the values in the last column):						

Weekly Scoring Worksheet (Week 17)

Your teacher will help you to fill in the numerical values for scoring criteria in the top row.

Player	Number of Goals × _____	Number of Saves and Assists × _____	Number of Yellow Cards and Red Cards × _____	Number of Total Shots by Player's Team × _____	Number of Fouls and Offsides by Player's Team × _____	Total Points for Player and Player's Team × _____
Total points (the sum of the values in the last column):						

Weekly Scoring Worksheet (Week 18)

Your teacher will help you to fill in the numerical values for scoring criteria in the top row.

Player	Number of Goals × _____	Number of Saves and Assists × _____	Number of Yellow Cards and Red Cards × _____	Number of Total Shots by Player's Team × _____	Number of Fouls and Offsides by Player's Team × _____	Total Points for Player and Player's Team × _____
Total points (the sum of the values in the last column):						

Weekly Scoring Worksheet (Week 19)

Your teacher will help you to fill in the numerical values for scoring criteria in the top row.

Player	Number of Goals × _____	Number of Saves and Assists × _____	Number of Yellow Cards and Red Cards × _____	Number of Total Shots by Player's Team × _____	Number of Fouls and Offsides by Player's Team × _____	Total Points for Player and Player's Team × _____
Total points (the sum of the values in the last column):						

Weekly Scoring Worksheet (Week 20)

Your teacher will help you to fill in the numerical values for scoring criteria in the top row.

Player	Number of Goals × _____	Number of Saves and Assists × _____	Number of Yellow Cards and Red Cards × _____	Number of Total Shots by Player's Team × _____	Number of Fouls and Offsides by Player's Team × _____	Total Points for Player and Player's Team × _____
Total points (the sum of the values in the last column):						

Weekly Scoring Worksheet (Week 21)

Your teacher will help you to fill in the numerical values for scoring criteria in the top row.

Player	Number of Goals × _____	Number of Saves and Assists × _____	Number of Yellow Cards and Red Cards × _____	Number of Total Shots by Player's Team × _____	Number of Fouls and Offsides by Player's Team × _____	Total Points for Player and Player's Team × _____
Total points (the sum of the values in the last column):						

Fantasy Soccer and Mathematics handouts

Weekly Scoring Worksheet (Week 22)

Your teacher will help you to fill in the numerical values for scoring criteria in the top row.

Player	Number of Goals × _____	Number of Saves and Assists × _____	Number of Yellow Cards and Red Cards × _____	Number of Total Shots by Player's Team × _____	Number of Fouls and Offsides by Player's Team × _____	Total Points for Player and Player's Team × _____
Total points (the sum of the values in the last column):						

Weekly Scoring Worksheet (Week 23)

Your teacher will help you to fill in the numerical values for scoring criteria in the top row.

Player	Number of Goals × _____	Number of Saves and Assists × _____	Number of Yellow Cards and Red Cards × _____	Number of Total Shots by Player's Team × _____	Number of Fouls and Offsides by Player's Team × _____	Total Points for Player and Player's Team × _____
Total points (the sum of the values in the last column):						

Fantasy Soccer and Mathematics handouts

Weekly Scoring Worksheet (Week 24)

Your teacher will help you to fill in the numerical values for scoring criteria in the top row.

Player	Number of Goals × _____	Number of Saves and Assists × _____	Number of Yellow Cards and Red Cards × _____	Number of Total Shots by Player's Team × _____	Number of Fouls and Offsides by Player's Team × _____	Total Points for Player and Player's Team × _____
Total points (the sum of the values in the last column):						

Peer Signature: _____

Weekly Scoring Worksheet (Week 25)

Your teacher will help you to fill in the numerical values for scoring criteria in the top row.

Player	Number of Goals × _____	Number of Saves and Assists × _____	Number of Yellow Cards and Red Cards × _____	Number of Total Shots by Player's Team × _____	Number of Fouls and Offsides by Player's Team × _____	Total Points for Player and Player's Team × _____

Total points (the sum of the values in the last column):

Weekly Scoring Worksheet (Week 26)

Your teacher will help you to fill in the numerical values for scoring criteria in the top row.

Player	Number of Goals × _____	Number of Saves and Assists × _____	Number of Yellow Cards and Red Cards × _____	Number of Total Shots by Player's Team × _____	Number of Fouls and Offsides by Player's Team × _____	Total Points for Player and Player's Team × _____
Total points (the sum of the values in the last column):						

Weekly Scoring Worksheet (Week 27)

Your teacher will help you to fill in the numerical values for scoring criteria in the top row.

Player	Number of Goals × _____	Number of Saves and Assists × _____	Number of Yellow Cards and Red Cards × _____	Number of Total Shots by Player's Team × _____	Number of Fouls and Offsides by Player's Team × _____	Total Points for Player and Player's Team × _____

Total points (the sum of the values in the last column):

Weekly Scoring Worksheet (Week 28)

Your teacher will help you to fill in the numerical values for scoring criteria in the top row.

Player	Number of Goals ✕ _____	Number of Saves and Assists ✕ _____	Number of Yellow Cards and Red Cards ✕ _____	Number of Total Shots by Player's Team ✕ _____	Number of Fouls and Offsides by Player's Team ✕ _____	Total Points for Player and Player's Team ✕ _____
Total points (the sum of the values in the last column):						

Weekly Scoring Worksheet (Week 29)

Your teacher will help you to fill in the numerical values for scoring criteria in the top row.

Player	Number of Goals × _____	Number of Saves and Assists × _____	Number of Yellow Cards and Red Cards × _____	Number of Total Shots by Player's Team × _____	Number of Fouls and Offsides by Player's Team × _____	Total Points for Player and Player's Team × _____
Total points (the sum of the values in the last column):						

Weekly Scoring Worksheet (Week 30)

Your teacher will help you to fill in the numerical values for scoring criteria in the top row.

Player	Number of Goals × _____	Number of Saves and Assists × _____	Number of Yellow Cards and Red Cards × _____	Number of Total Shots by Player's Team × _____	Number of Fouls and Offsides by Player's Team × _____	Total Points for Player and Player's Team × _____
Total points (the sum of the values in the last column):						

HANDOUT 10

Weekly Scoring Worksheet Using Total Points Equations (Week 1)

Write the total points equation you use in the box below. Then compute the points for each of your players.

Player	Computation	Points
Total points (the sum of the values in the last column):		

Weekly Scoring Worksheet Using Total Points Equations (Week 2)

Write the total points equation you use in the box below. Then compute the points for each of your players.

Player	Computation	Points
Total points (the sum of the values in the last column):		

Weekly Scoring Worksheet Using Total Points Equations (Week 3)

Write the total points equation you use in the box below. Then compute the points for each of your players.

Player	Computation	Points
Total points (the sum of the values in the last column):		

Weekly Scoring Worksheet Using Total Points Equations (Week 4)

Write the total points equation you use in the box below. Then compute the points for each of your players.

Player	Computation	Points
Total points (the sum of the values in the last column):		

Weekly Scoring Worksheet Using Total Points Equations (Week 5)

Write the total points equation you use in the box below. Then compute the points for each of your players.

Player	Computation	Points
Total points (the sum of the values in the last column):		

Weekly Scoring Worksheet Using Total Points Equations (Week 6)

Write the total points equation you use in the box below. Then compute the points for each of your players.

Player	Computation	Points
Total points (the sum of the values in the last column):		

Weekly Scoring Worksheet Using Total Points Equations (Week 7)

Write the total points equation you use in the box below. Then compute the points for each of your players.

Player	Computation	Points
Total points (the sum of the values in the last column):		

Fantasy Soccer and Mathematics handouts

Weekly Scoring Worksheet Using Total Points Equations (Week 8)

Write the total points equation you use in the box below. Then compute the points for each of your players.

Player	Computation	Points
Total points (the sum of the values in the last column):		

Weekly Scoring Worksheet Using Total Points Equations (Week 9)

Write the total points equation you use in the box below. Then compute the points for each of your players.

Player	Computation	Points
Total points (the sum of the values in the last column):		

Weekly Scoring Worksheet Using Total Points Equations (Week 10)

Write the total points equation you use in the box below. Then compute the points for each of your players.

Player	Computation	Points
Total points (the sum of the values in the last column):		

Weekly Scoring Worksheet Using Total Points Equations (Week 11)

Write the total points equation you use in the box below. Then compute the points for each of your players.

| | | |

Player	Computation	Points
Total points (the sum of the values in the last column):		

Weekly Scoring Worksheet Using Total Points Equations (Week 12)

Write the total points equation you use in the box below. Then compute the points for each of your players.

Player	Computation	Points
Total points (the sum of the values in the last column):		

Weekly Scoring Worksheet Using Total Points Equations (Week 13)

Write the total points equation you use in the box below. Then compute the points for each of your players.

Player	Computation	Points
Total points (the sum of the values in the last column):		

Weekly Scoring Worksheet Using Total Points Equations (Week 14)

Write the total points equation you use in the box below. Then compute the points for each of your players.

Player	Computation	Points
Total points (the sum of the values in the last column):		

Weekly Scoring Worksheet Using Total Points Equations (Week 15)

Write the total points equation you use in the box below. Then compute the points for each of your players.

Player	Computation	Points
Total points (the sum of the values in the last column):		

Fantasy Soccer and Mathematics handouts

Weekly Scoring Worksheet Using Total Points Equations (Week 16)

Write the total points equation you use in the box below. Then compute the points for each of your players.

Player	Computation	Points
Total points (the sum of the values in the last column):		

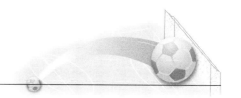

Weekly Scoring Worksheet Using Total Points Equations (Week 17)

Write the total points equation you use in the box below. Then compute the points for each of your players.

Player	Computation	Points
Total points (the sum of the values in the last column):		

Weekly Scoring Worksheet Using Total Points Equations (Week 18)

Write the total points equation you use in the box below. Then compute the points for each of your players.

Player	Computation	Points
Total points (the sum of the values in the last column):		

Weekly Scoring Worksheet Using Total Points Equations (Week 19)

Write the total points equation you use in the box below. Then compute the points for each of your players.

Player	Computation	Points
Total points (the sum of the values in the last column):		

Weekly Scoring Worksheet Using Total Points Equations (Week 20)

Write the total points equation you use in the box below. Then compute the points for each of your players.

Player	Computation	Points
Total points (the sum of the values in the last column):		

Weekly Scoring Worksheet Using Total Points Equations (Week 21)

Write the total points equation you use in the box below. Then compute the points for each of your players.

Player	Computation	Points
Total points (the sum of the values in the last column):		

Weekly Scoring Worksheet Using Total Points Equations (Week 22)

Write the total points equation you use in the box below. Then compute the points for each of your players.

Player	Computation	Points
Total points (the sum of the values in the last column):		

Weekly Scoring Worksheet Using Total Points Equations (Week 23)

Write the total points equation you use in the box below. Then compute the points for each of your players.

Player	Computation	Points
Total points (the sum of the values in the last column):		

Weekly Scoring Worksheet Using Total Points Equations (Week 24)

Write the total points equation you use in the box below. Then compute the points for each of your players.

Player	Computation	Points
Total points (the sum of the values in the last column):		

Weekly Scoring Worksheet Using Total Points Equations (Week 25)

Write the total points equation you use in the box below. Then compute the points for each of your players.

Player	Computation	Points
Total points (the sum of the values in the last column):		

Fantasy Soccer and Mathematics handouts

Weekly Scoring Worksheet Using Total Points Equations (Week 26)

Write the total points equation you use in the box below. Then compute the points for each of your players.

Player	Computation	Points
Total points (the sum of the values in the last column):		

Weekly Scoring Worksheet Using Total Points Equations (Week 27)

Write the total points equation you use in the box below. Then compute the points for each of your players.

Player	Computation	Points
Total points (the sum of the values in the last column):		

Weekly Scoring Worksheet Using Total Points Equations (Week 28)

Write the total points equation you use in the box below. Then compute the points for each of your players.

Player	Computation	Points
Total points (the sum of the values in the last column):		

Weekly Scoring Worksheet Using Total Points Equations (Week 29)

Write the total points equation you use in the box below. Then compute the points for each of your players.

Player	Computation	Points
Total points (the sum of the values in the last column):		

Weekly Scoring Worksheet Using Total Points Equations (Week 30)

Write the total points equation you use in the box below. Then compute the points for each of your players.

Player	Computation	Points
Total points (the sum of the values in the last column):		

Total Points Week-by-Week

Team Name: _____   Student Name: _____

Player	Week 1	Week 2	Week 3	Week 4	Week 5	Week 6

Weekly total _____

Cumulative total _____

Total Points Week-by-Week *(Cont'd.)*

Team Name: _____   Student Name: _____

Player	Week 7	Week 8	Week 9	Week 10	Week 11	Week 12

Weekly total _____

Cumulative total _____

Total Points Week-by-Week *(Cont'd.)*

Team Name: _____   Student Name: _____

Player	Week 13	Week 14	Week 15	Week 16	Week 17	Week 18

Weekly total _____

Cumulative total _____

Fantasy Soccer and Mathematics handouts

Total Points Week-by-Week *(Cont'd.)*

Team Name: _____   Student Name: _____

Player	Week 19	Week 20	Week 21	Week 22	Week 23	Week 24

Weekly total _____

Cumulative total _____

Total Points Week-by-Week *(Cont'd.)*

Team Name: _____   Student Name: _____

Player	Week 25	Week 26	Week 27	Week 28	Week 29	Week 30

Weekly total _____

Cumulative total _____

Fantasy Soccer and Mathematics handouts

Graphing Activities

Graphing

Every week, choose three players from your team, and record their weekly points on circle, stacked-bar, or multiple-line graphs.

Circle Graphs

Circle graphs indicate the percentage of your fantasy team's points scored by each player. The equation for computing the measurement of a central angle is as follows:

$$W \div S \times 360 = A$$

W = total weekly points for one player and his or her team
S = total weekly points for a student's fantasy team
A = the measurement of the central angle on the circle graph

Figure 3.1. Circle Graph

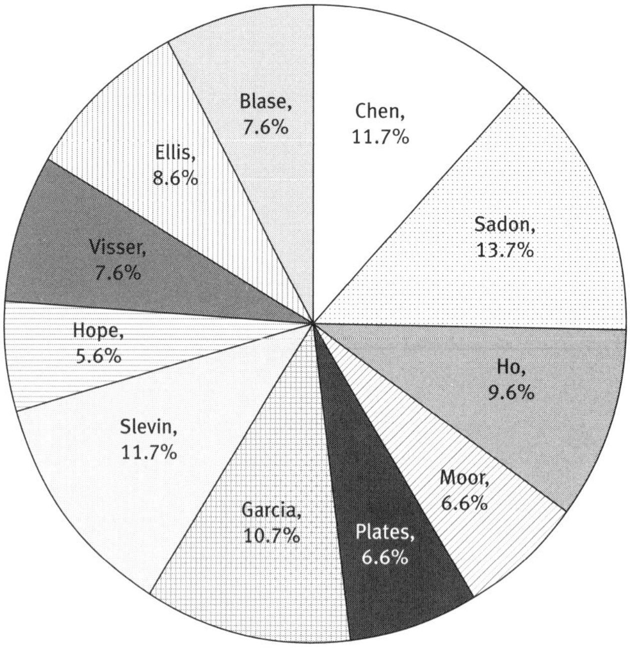

Panthers Scoring Breakdown, Week 1

Example:

Yi Chen's total points for week 1 (in simplest form):

$$W = \frac{23}{24}$$

$$S = 8\frac{5}{24}$$

Thus, $\frac{23}{24} \div 8\frac{5}{24} \times 360 = A$

$$A = 42°$$

Figure 3.1 shows a circle graph of the points breakdown for the Panthers in week 1.

Stacked-Bar and Multiple-Line Graphs

Points earned by individual players can be shown on stacked-bar graphs and multiple-line graphs. A stacked-bar graph is a bar graph in which players' weekly points are "stacked" on top of each other. Multiple-line graphs are line graphs that depict the weekly points earned by two or more players. Examples of these graphs are found on the following pages. Intervals of $\frac{2}{24}$ for the stacked-bar graphs and $\frac{1}{24}$ for the multiple-line graphs work well if you are using the default scoring system. You may need to tape a second sheet of graph paper to the top of your first sheet in order to accommodate weeks in which their players accumulate significant points.

The following pages contain examples of computer-generated graphs.

Stacked-Bar Graph

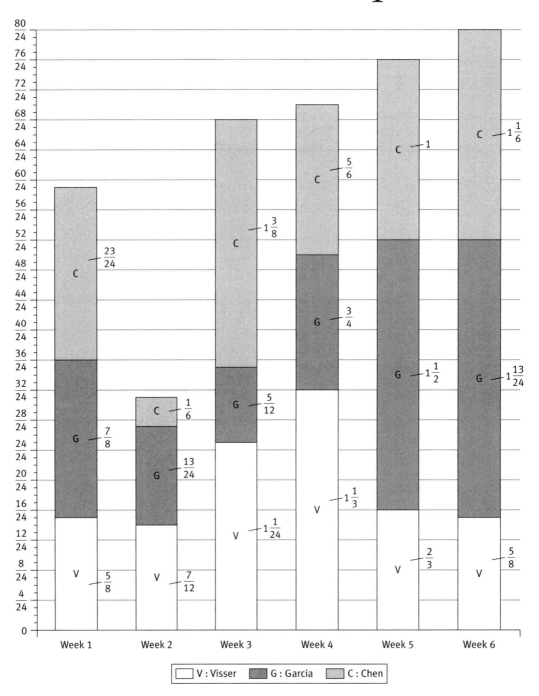

Panthers Scoring Breakdown, Weeks 1–6

Graphing

Multiple-Line Graph

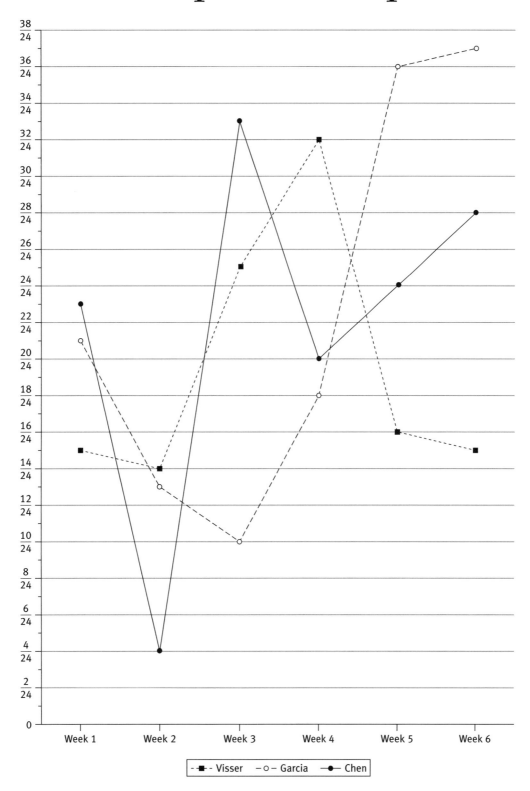

Panthers Scoring Breakdown, Weeks 1–6

Graphing

Practice Worksheets

Name _____

Rounding Whole Numbers and Expanded Notation

1. Round the following player salaries to the units given. The first line gives an example.

Salary	Nearest $10,000	Nearest $100,000	Nearest $1,000,000
$22,200,350	22,200,000	22,200,000	22,000,000
$ 3,444,505			
$ 9,800,800			
$ 5,555,555			
$12,000,825			

2. Use expanded notation to represent the following player salaries. The first line gives an example.

Salary

$ 6,675,500 = 6,000,000 + 600,000 + 70,000 + 5,000 + 500

$16,222,900

$ 1,775,050

$14,129,034

$11,746,632

$13,999,999

Name _____

Least Common Multiple
and Greatest Common Factor

The number of goals and fouls for five players during the first half of the season are listed below. Find the least common multiple and greatest common factor for each pair of numbers. The first line gives an example.

Player	Goals and Fouls	Least Common Multiple	Greatest Common Factor
Player A	11, 44	44	11
Player B	24, 36		
Player C	16, 40		
Player D	14, 35		
Player E	8, 20		

Number sense

Name _____

Operations with Whole Numbers

1. What is the difference between the highest and lowest salary for the players listed below?

Isabella Garcia	$27,800,000
Hannah Thompson	$16,555,935
Kalisha Jackson	$25,675,225
Maria Giuseppe	$38,000,810
Heng Huang	$ 3,300,900

2. What is the total cost of the players listed in question 1?

3. What is the average salary of the players listed in question 1 to the nearest dollar?

4. If Emilio Martinez had 165 saves in 15 games, how many saves did he average per game?

5. If 13 soccer players each have a salary of $2.75 million, what is the sum of their salaries?

Number sense

Name _____

Equivalent Fractions

The weekly points earned by players on the Panthers are listed below. List the first three equivalent fractions for each. The first line gives an example.

Yi Chen $\frac{5}{6}$ $\frac{10}{12}$ $\frac{15}{18}$ $\frac{20}{24}$

Jorge Sadon $\frac{3}{5}$ _____ _____ _____

Ming Ho $\frac{7}{24}$ _____ _____ _____

Brian Moor $\frac{7}{8}$ _____ _____ _____

Denzel Plates $\frac{7}{12}$ _____ _____ _____

Pedro Garcia $\frac{2}{3}$ _____ _____ _____

Livan Slevin $\frac{3}{4}$ _____ _____ _____

Number sense

Name _____

Patterns and Multiples

(Use with Handout 12)

1. Find the first three multiples for the points earned by Lars Visser for Week 2. The first line gives an example.

2. Find the second and fourth multiples for the points earned by Yi Chen for Week 4.

3. Find the third and fifth multiples for the points earned by Pedro Garcia for Week 4.

4. If $\frac{15}{12}$ is the third multiple of a number, what is the original number?

5. If $\frac{14}{12}$ is the seventh multiple of a number, what is the original number?

Number sense

Name _____

Ordering Fractions and Decimals

(Use with Handout 12)

Example

For weeks 3–4, use inequalities to arrange the weekly points earned by Lars Visser, Pedro Garcia, and Yi Chen in ascending order.

$$\frac{5}{12} < \frac{3}{4} < \frac{5}{6} < 1\frac{1}{24} < 1\frac{1}{3} < 1\frac{3}{8}$$

After converting the fractions to decimals and rounding to the nearest thousandth, arrange the decimals in descending order. Thus,

$$1.375 > 1.333 > 1.042 > .833 > .750 > .417$$

1. Use inequalities and fractions to arrange in descending order the cumulative points earned by Visser, Garcia, and Chen for weeks 1–3.

2. Use inequalities and decimals to arrange in ascending order the cumulative points earned by Visser, Garcia, and Chen for weeks 2–4. Round decimals to the nearest thousandth.

Number sense

PRACTICE WORKSHEET 7

Rounding Decimals

(Use with Handout 12)

Round each player's cumulative points from weeks 1–6 to the nearest tenth, hundredth, and thousandth.

Example

Livan Slevin's cumulative points for weeks 1–6: $4.458\overline{3}$

  Round to the nearest tenth = 4.5

  Round to the nearest hundredth = 4.46

  Round to the nearest thousandth = 4.458

Table 1

	Visser	Garcia	Chen
Cumulative points			
Nearest tenth			
Nearest hundredth			
Nearest thousandth			

Use the following table to round the cumulative points for your top three players for weeks 1–6.

Table 2

	Player 1	Player 2	Player 3
Cumulative points			
Nearest tenth			
Nearest hundredth			
Nearest thousandth			

Number sense

Name _____

Improper Fractions, Mixed Numbers, and Reciprocals

The weekly point totals for a team are listed below. Convert all improper fractions to mixed numbers, and write each in its simplest form.

Example

$$\frac{203}{24} = 8\frac{11}{24}$$

1. $\dfrac{267}{24}$

2. $\dfrac{180}{24}$

3. $\dfrac{155}{24}$

4. $\dfrac{139}{24}$

5. $\dfrac{199}{24}$

Write the reciprocals (in simplest form) of the original fractions given in problems 1–5.

6.

7.

8.

9.

10.

Number sense

Name _____

Adding and Subtracting Fractions

(Use with Handout 12)

Example

For week 5, find the sum of the points earned by Lars Visser, Pedro Garcia, and Yi Chen.

$$\frac{2}{3} + 1\frac{1}{2} + 1 = \frac{76}{24} = 3\frac{4}{24} = 3\frac{1}{6}$$

1. For weeks 3 and 4, find the sum of the points earned by Lars Visser, Pedro Garcia, and Yi Chen.

2. How many fewer points did the Panthers earn during weeks 1–3 compared to weeks 4–6?

3. Find the sum of the points earned by Pedro Garcia and Yi Chen for weeks 1–5.

4. How many more cumulative points did Yi Chen earn compared to Lars Visser?

5. How many fewer cumulative points did Pedro Garcia earn in weeks 2–4 compared to Lars Visser during the same period?

Number sense

Name _____

Stacked–Bar Graphs

Using graph paper, construct a stacked-bar graph based on the data below. *Hint:* Convert all fractions into a common denominator.

Player	Week 1	Week 2	Week 3
Freda Schleiermacher	$\dfrac{1}{6}$	$\dfrac{7}{24}$	$\dfrac{11}{24}$
Reynaldo Fuentes	$\dfrac{3}{8}$	$\dfrac{1}{3}$	$\dfrac{1}{4}$
Lian Ng	$\dfrac{5}{24}$	$\dfrac{19}{24}$	$\dfrac{1}{2}$

Number sense

Multiplying and Dividing Fractions

(Use with Handout 12)

1. How many weeks would it take Brian Moor to earn $9\frac{1}{3}$ points if he averaged $1\frac{1}{3}$ points a week?

2. What is the product of the points earned by Pedro Garcia for weeks 4 and 5?

3. The product of the points earned by Lars Visser for weeks 3 and 4 is $1\frac{7}{18}$. If Visser earned $1\frac{1}{3}$ points for week 4, how many points did he earn for week 3?

4. Rinalo Ellis earned $17\frac{1}{4}$ points during the first 23 weeks of the season. How many points did he average per week?

5. If Carmelo Blase earned $20\frac{1}{4}$ points for the season and Denzel Plates averaged $\frac{1}{8}$ for each week, how many weeks would it take Plates to match Blase?

Number sense

PRACTICE WORKSHEET 12

Rounding Fractions

(Use with Handout 12)

Round players' cumulative points from weeks 1–6 to the nearest $\frac{1}{2}$, $\frac{1}{4}$, and $\frac{1}{8}$.

Example

Rinalo Ellis's cumulative points for weeks 1–6 = $3\frac{11}{24}$

Round to the nearest $\frac{1}{2} = 3\frac{1}{2}$

Round to the nearest $\frac{1}{4} = 3\frac{2}{4}$

Round to the nearest $\frac{1}{8} = 3\frac{4}{8}$

Table 1

	Visser	Garcia	Chen
Cumulative points			
Nearest $\frac{1}{2}$			
Nearest $\frac{1}{4}$			
Nearest $\frac{1}{8}$			

Use the following table to round the cumulative points for your players for weeks 1–6.

Table 2

Nearest	Player A	Player B	Player C
Cumulative points			
$\frac{1}{2}$			
$\frac{1}{4}$			
$\frac{1}{8}$			

Number sense

Multiplying and Dividing Decimals

1. Bao Wang averaged 5.8 saves per game for 29 games. Her annual salary is $1,250,000. How much did she earn per save for the season?

2. If Xiao Xia worked 8 hours a day, 175 days a year, and her annual salary was $1.65 million, how much money did she make each working day? Each working hour? Each working minute? Each working second? Round your answer to the nearest cent.

3. If a snail can crawl at a rate of .035 yards per minute, how many hours will it take the snail to crawl the length of a soccer field (390 feet)? One mile?

4. If 43,000 fans each consumed an average of 10.15 ounces of soda at each game, how many ounces of soda were consumed at 5 games?

5. If a vendor selling ice cream sandwiches works 3.5 hours at $7.35 an hour and also receives 29 cents for each sandwich sold, what is her income if she sold 302 ice cream sandwiches?

Number sense

Name _____

Unit Rates

Example

At a soccer game, you can purchase 12 ounces of soda for $3.75 or 18 ounces for $5.25. Which size costs less per ounce?

$$\$3.75 \div 12 \text{ oz.} = 31 \text{ cents per ounce}$$
$$\$5.25 \div 18 \text{ oz.} = 29 \text{ cents per ounce}$$

1. You can purchase a 14-ounce bag of peanuts for $3.60 or a 20 ounce bag for $4.60. Which size bag costs less per ounce?

2. If Amber De Jong drove her car 400 miles on 16 gallons of gas and Blake Janssen drove her car 380 miles on 13 gallons of gas, how many miles per gallon does each car get?

3. If Dulce Gonzalez can purchase 12 acres for $36 million or 20 acres for $55 million, what is the cost of the lower price per acre?

4. If you can purchase a 15-game season ticket for $400 or a 1-game ticket for $30, which is the lower price per game?

5. What is the higher salary per year: $28 million for 13 years or $35 million for 18 years?

Number sense

Converting Fractions, Decimals, and Percentages

(Use with Handout 12)

1. Find the cumulative points for each player, and convert the fractions into decimals. Then round to the nearest tenth, hundredth, and thousandth. Finally, convert all decimals to a percentage, rounded to the nearest tenth. The first row is filled in as an example.

	Total Points, Fraction	Total Points, Decimal	Rounded to Nearest Tenth	Rounded to Nearest Hundredth	Rounded to Nearest Thousandth	Percentage to Nearest Tenth
Visser	$4\frac{7}{8}$	4.875	4.9	4.88	4.875	487.5%
Garcia						
Chen						

Number sense

Converting Fractions, Decimals, and Percentages *(Cont'd.)*

2. Fill in the table below for the cumulative points for your team for the first six weeks.

Your Players	Total Points, Fraction	Total Points, Decimal	Rounded to Nearest Tenth	Rounded to Nearest Hundredth	Rounded to Nearest Thousandth	Percentage (Rounded to Nearest Tenth)

Name _____

Ratios

(Use with Handout 12)

Express the following ratios in decimal format to the nearest thousandth.

   1. Cumulative points for Chen and Visser compared to cumulative points for Garcia.

   2. Cumulative points for Visser compared to cumulative points for Chen.

   3. Cumulative points for Garcia compared to cumulative points for Visser.

   4. Cumulative points for Chen compared to cumulative points for Visser and Garcia.

   5. Cumulative points for Chen and Garcia compared to cumulative points for Visser.

Name _____

Percentage of Price Increase and Decrease

Example

If the price of a soccer jersey rose from $40 to $48, what is the percentage of price increase?

$$\frac{\text{Change in Price}}{\text{Original Price}} = \frac{8}{40} = .2 = 20\% \text{ increase}$$

1. If the price of a soccer ball autographed by Cai Phan rose from $120 to $145, what is the percentage of price increase?

2. If the price of a soccer video game decreased from $36 to $29, what is the percentage of price decrease?

3. If the price of a season ticket decreased from $415 to $375, what is the percentage of price decrease?

4. If the price of a season ticket increased from $365 to $440, what is the percentage of price increase?

5. If the combined salaries for all players on a soccer team increased from $130 million to $150 million, what percentage increase would that represent?

Number sense

PRACTICE WORKSHEET 18

Finding a Percentage of a Number

Example

Larisa Shishkova earned $1\frac{13}{24}$ points while Margarita Ryzhkov earned $\frac{1}{2}$ points. What percentage of Shishkova's points do Ryzhkov's points represent?

$$n \times 1\frac{13}{24} = \frac{1}{2}$$

$$\text{therefore, } n = \frac{1}{2} \div 1\frac{13}{24}$$

$$\text{thus, } n = \frac{24}{74} = .324 = 32.4\%$$

1. Frida Olsson earned $\frac{7}{8}$ points, while Greta Bengtsson earned $1\frac{5}{12}$ points. What percentage of Bengtsson's points do Olsson's points represent?

2. Carlos Villa earned $1\frac{17}{24}$ points, while Elena Popa earned $\frac{5}{6}$ points. What percentage of Villa's points do Popa's points represent?

3. Helga Dumitrescu earned $3\frac{1}{8}$ points, while Jeff Manchester earned 4 points. What percentage of Dumitrescu's points do Manchester's points represent?

4. Camila Azevedo earned $2\frac{2}{3}$ points, which was 25% of Adelina Mendes's points. How many points did Mendes earn?

Number sense

Finding a Percentage of a Number *(Cont'd.)*

5. Elise Benoit earned $\frac{5}{24}$ points, which was 25% of George Adam's points. How many points did Adam earn?

6. Hector Ortiz earned $2\frac{3}{4}$ points, which was 150% of Mariano Martinez's points. How many points did Martinez earn?

7. If Shawn Wagner earned 150% of $2\frac{1}{6}$ points, how many points did he earn?

8. There are 2,000 Husky fans in Fortuna and 500 Bear fans in Scotia. Each year, 5% of the Husky fans move to Scotia, and 10% of the Bear fans move to Fortuna. Complete the table below.

After Year	Husky Fans in Fortuna	Bear Fans in Scotia
1		
2		
3		
4		

Number sense

Name _____

Proportions

Example

If Reynaldo Lopez earned $2\frac{3}{4}$ points for his first 3 games of the season, how many points is he projected to earn for 9 games?

$$\frac{2.75}{3} = \frac{n}{9}$$

$$2.75(9) = 3n$$

$$n = 8.25$$

1. If Links O'Brady earned $11\frac{11}{12}$ points during the first half of the season, how many points is he projected to earn for a thirty-game season?

2. If it took Shea O'Malley 12 weeks to earn 9 points, how many weeks would it take him to earn $5\frac{1}{4}$ points?

3. An architect is constructing a scale drawing of a new soccer stadium. On the scale, 1 inch represents 50 feet. If the length of the actual field is 300 feet, what is the length of the field on the scale drawing?

4. Stan Lowe earned $4\frac{1}{6}$ points for 10 weeks. If he earned an equal number of points each week, how many points would he have accumulated after 8 weeks?

Number sense

Name _____

Ratios and Proportions

Example

The ratio of Cho Yamamoto's points to Aleksander Jonas's points is 3:2. If Yamamoto earned 1.5 points, how many points did Jonas earn?

$$\frac{3}{2} = \frac{1 \cdot 5}{n}$$

$$3n = 2(1.5)$$

$$3n = 3$$

$$n = 1$$

1. The ratio of Sheets Cairn's points to Basil Benjamin's points is 4:3. If Cairns earned 1.5 points, how many points did Benjamin earn?

2. The ratio of Philippe Laflour's points to Jordana Garcia's points is 1:3. If Garcia earned $\frac{5}{8}$ points, how many points did Laflour earn?

3. The ratio of Juanita Gonzalez's points to Christina Hernandez's points is 5:2. If Gonzalez earned 1.25 points, how many points did Hernandez earn?

4. The ratio of Ben Lewis's points to William Roberts's points is 6:5. If Roberts earned 9 points, how many points did Lewis earn?

5. The ratio of Ishi Tanaka's points to Lashanna Williams's points is 7:24. If Tanaka earned 21 points, how many points did Williams earn?

Number sense

Name _____

Factoring

Example

The product of the points earned by Yolanda Davis for weeks 1 and 2 is $1\frac{1}{24}$. If Davis earned $1\frac{2}{3}$ points for week 1, how many points did she earn for week 2?

$$\frac{5}{3} \times \frac{\square}{\square} = \frac{25}{24}$$

$$n = \frac{5}{8}$$

1. The product of the points earned by Jada Brown and Morgan Bach is 1. If Brown earned $\frac{21}{32}$ points, how many points did Bach earn?

2. Find two factors whose product equals $\frac{21}{32}$.

3. The area of a parking lot is 300,000 square feet. If the length and width are whole numbers, what are the most realistic factors for the dimensions of the parking lot?

4. One factor of $\frac{18}{24}$ is $\frac{3}{6}$. Find a second factor.

5. Find a second factor if one factor of $\frac{5}{10}$ is $\frac{2}{4}$.

Number sense

Name _____

Interest, Depreciation, and Tax

1. If a player signed a five-year contract for $70,000,000 and invested 10% of his annual salary at a rate of 6.25%, how much interest will he earn at the end of two years if the interest is compounded annually? (Assume that his income remains constant during the life of the contract.) Construct a spreadsheet showing the interest earned and total value of his account at the end of each year. Use the following formula:

   I = PRT
   I = interest earned
   P = principle
   R = interest rate
   T = time

2. If a player purchased a car for $260,000 and the state sales tax rate is 7.75%, how much tax will she owe? What will be the total cost of the car?

3. If the price of the automobile, excluding tax, in problem 2 depreciates by 12% each year, what will be the value of the car at the end of 2 years? Construct a spreadsheet showing the amount of depreciation and corresponding value of the car each year.

4. If a player purchased a house for $8,900,000, and the price of the home appreciates 7% a year for the next two years, what will be the value of the home at the end of that period? Construct a spreadsheet showing the amount of annual appreciation and corresponding value of the house at the end of each year.

Number sense

PRACTICE WORKSHEET 23

Prime Factorization

1. Below are the weekly point totals (in 24ths) for a team. Write the prime factorization of each number using exponential notation. The first row is filled in as an example.

Week	Point Totals	Prime Factorization
Week 1	120	$2^3 \times 3 \times 5$
Week 2	89	
Week 3	81	
Week 4	144	
Week 5	188	
Week 6	66	
Week 7	53	

2. List the first five prime numbers: _____ _____ _____ _____ _____

Number sense

Name _____

Scientific Notation

The rectangular dimensions of a soccer training facility are 600 by 1,500 feet. Write the area in scientific notation for the following units of measurement. *Hint:* 1 in. = 2.5 cm.

Example

Square feet   Area = $600 \times 1,500 = 900,000$ sq. ft. = 9.0×10^5

   1. Square inches

   2. Square yards

   3. Square centimeters

   4. Square millimeters

   5. Square meters

Write the following in scientific notation.

   6. 702.5711

   7. .00000006

   8. .300001

   9. 992,844.522

  10. 34,360,944.8

Write the following in standard form.

  11. 653.0003×10^{-2}

  12. $56\dfrac{3}{8} \times 10^3$

Name _____

Ordering Integers, Fractions, and Decimals

1. The following integers represent December temperatures for several cities that host soccer teams. Place them in ascending order on the number line below.

   23   −8   −14   −4   75   22   41   56   34   −12   51

2. The following integers represent the weekly points earned (in 24ths) by a player during the first 10 games of the season. Place them in ascending order on the number line below.

   −16   22   25   −11   −25   −12   −21   −8   13   −3

3. Place the following numerical values on the number line in ascending order.

   $-.19934$ $11\frac{7}{12}$ $-2\frac{23}{24}$ -5.09 5.123 -5.123

4. On the number line below, place the following point totals in ascending order.

   $\frac{5}{12}$ $\frac{13}{24}$ $\frac{5}{6}$ $.0717$ $\frac{7}{8}$ $.7017$ $.1707$

Number sense

Name _____

Operations with Integers

1. If a player scored 169 goals in 13 seasons, how many goals did he average per season?

2. The numerical values below represent the points earned for 10 players. How many total points did they gain or lose?

-26 18 -19 39 32 -31 31 -13 13 -22

3. If a player earned -11 points for the first one-tenth of the season, how many points is he projected to lose for a whole season?

4. If a goalkeeper had 105 saves in 15 games, how many saves did he average per game?

5. The numbers below represent profit or loss for five teams for one year. What is the average profit or loss?

$-\$335,000$ $\$11,646,522$ $\$6,723,311$ $-\$716,829$ $-\$19,776,700$

Number sense

Operations with Integers *(Cont'd.)*

6. If one team lost $8,978,602 while another team reported a profit of $21,656,800, how much greater was one team's profit compared to the other team's loss?

7. If one team reported a loss of $2,111,445, which included a profit of $1,777,338 on parking fees, how much money did it lose on operations other than parking fees?

Name _____

Permutations and Combinations

1. There are seven midfielders on a team. If the coach started three midfielders, how many combinations could he choose from?

2. If a team has jerseys in four different styles, shoes in two different styles, and pants in three different styles, how many combinations of uniforms are there to choose from?

3. A soccer team's uniform consist of four colors, but they have six colors to choose from. How many combinations of uniforms do they have?

4. Before a game, four referees line up in single file for the National Anthem. In how many ways can the referees line up in single file?

Number sense

Name _____

Unit Conversions

1. The distance between goal lines on a soccer field is 130 yards. What is this distance in inches? In centimeters? (2.5 centimeters = 1 inch)

2. If a player scored 14 goals from an average distance of 23 feet, how many inches did the ball travel for all 23 goals?

3. The distance between touch lines on a soccer field is 225 feet. What is this distance in yards? In inches?

4. The length of the coaching and team area on a soccer field is 20 yards. What is this distance in centimeters? In millimeters? *Hint:* 10 mm = 1 cm.

5. A team spent 2,765 minutes practicing last week. How many hours did they spend practicing?

6. A team's next game is in exactly 2 days, 14 hours. How many hours until they play their next game? How many minutes?

Algebra and functions

Name _____

Evaluating Algebraic Expressions

Evaluate $\dfrac{1}{4}(G) + \dfrac{1}{6}(S + A) - \dfrac{1}{12}(Y + R) + \dfrac{1}{8}(T) - \dfrac{1}{24}(F + O)$ if:

1. $G = 1$
   $S = 2$
   $A = 1$
   $Y = 0$
   $R = 0$
   $T = 12$
   $F = 17$
   $O = 3$

2. $G = 2$
   $S = 3$
   $A = 0$
   $Y = 1$
   $R = 0$
   $T = 13$
   $F = 17$
   $O = 4$

3. $G = 1$
   $S = 2$
   $A = 2$
   $Y = 2$
   $R = 1$
   $T = 7$
   $F = 19$
   $O = 5$

Algebra and functions

Name _____

Properties of Mathematics

Use numerical values to write one equation for each of the properties listed.

Distributive property	$a(b + c) = ab + ac$
Commutative property of addition	$a + b = b + a$
Commutative property of multiplication	$ab = ba$
Associative property of addition	$a + (b + c) = (a + b) + c$
Associative property of multiplication	$a(bc) = (ab)c$
Inverse property of addition	$a + (-a) = 0$
Inverse property of multiplication	$a\left(\dfrac{1}{a}\right) = 1$
Identity property of addition	$a + 0 = a$
Identity property of multiplication	$a(1) = a$

Property: _____

Property: _____

Property: _____

Property: _____

Property: _____

Property: _____

Property: _____

Property: _____

Property: _____

Algebra and functions

PRACTICE WORKSHEET 31

Graphing on a Number Line

(Use with Handout 12)

Example

During the first six weeks, Hui Zhang's range of points earned was between 0 and $1\frac{5}{8}$, inclusive. Using these data, we can graph Zhang's range of points earned on a number line:

$$\bullet\!\!-\!\!-\!\!-\!\!-\!\!-\!\!-\!\!-\!\!-\!\!\bullet$$

$$0 \qquad\qquad 1\frac{5}{8}$$

Use number lines to graph the range of points earned from weeks 2–5 for Yi Chen, Lars Visser, and Pedro Garcia.

Chen _____

Visser _____

Garcia _____

Algebra and functions

Linear Equations (A)

The equations below are used to compute total weekly points or to find the measurement of central angles in a circle graph. In each case, solve for the variable.

1. $\dfrac{1}{4}(G) + \dfrac{1}{6}(3 + 1) - \dfrac{1}{12}(1 + 0) + \dfrac{1}{8}(13) - \dfrac{1}{24}(21 + 7) = 1\dfrac{13}{24}$

2. $\dfrac{1}{4}(1) + \dfrac{1}{6}(S + 2) - \dfrac{1}{12}(2 + 1) + \dfrac{1}{8}(7) - \dfrac{1}{24}(11 + 5) = \dfrac{17}{24}$

3. $\dfrac{1}{4}(3) + \dfrac{1}{6}(3 + A) - 1\dfrac{5}{8}(1 + 0) + \dfrac{1}{8}(9) - \dfrac{1}{24}(12 + 4) = 1\dfrac{5}{8}$

4. $\dfrac{1}{4}(0) + \dfrac{1}{6}(2 + 1) - \dfrac{1}{12}(1 + 0) + \dfrac{1}{8}(T) - \dfrac{1}{24}(9 + 2) = 1\dfrac{11}{24}$

Algebra and functions

Linear Equations (A) *(Cont'd.)*

5. $\dfrac{w}{.75} \times 360 = 90$

6. $\dfrac{1}{4}(0) + \dfrac{1}{6}(8 + 0) - \dfrac{1}{12}(0 + 1) + \dfrac{1}{8}(7) - \dfrac{17}{24}(2 + O) = \dfrac{17}{24}$

7. $\dfrac{.25}{s} \times 360 = 1$

8. $\dfrac{1}{4}(3) + \dfrac{1}{6}(1 + 2) - \dfrac{1}{12}(1 + 1) + \dfrac{1}{8}(1) - \dfrac{5}{12}(F + O) = \dfrac{3}{8}$

Algebra and functions

Name _____

Linear Equations (B)

In the problems below, insert the variables into the total points equation. Then solve the problem, and write the answer in its simplest form.

$$\frac{1}{4}(G) + \frac{1}{6}(S + A) - \frac{1}{12}(Y + R) + \frac{1}{8}(T) - \frac{1}{24}(F + O) = W$$

1. $G = 2$
   $S = 3$
   $A = 1$
   $Y = 1$
   $R = 0$
   $T = 8$
   $F = 15$
   $O = 4$

2. $G = 1$
   $S = 3$
   $A = 0$
   $Y = 2$
   $R = 1$
   $T = 14$
   $F = 21$
   $O = 3$

3. $G = 0$
   $S = 11$
   $A = 0$
   $Y = 1$
   $R = 0$
   $T = 5$
   $F = 8$
   $O = 2$

Algebra and functions

Area and Perimeter of Rectangles

1. Explain the meaning of the variables in the following equations:

$$P = 2l + 2w$$

$$A = bh$$

2. The rectangular dimensions of two soccer stadiums are 1,150 feet by 900 feet and 980 feet by 800 feet, respectively. Then complete the table below. Do you see any patterns? Explain your answer.

	Area of First Stadium (1,150 ft. by 900 ft.)	Area of Second Stadium (980 ft. by 800 ft.)	Ratio of Area of First Stadium to Area of Second Stadium
Square feet			
Square inches			
Square yards			
Square centimeters (2.5 cm = 1 inch)			
Square millimeters			
Square meters			

3. If turf costs $105 per square foot, how much would it cost to resurface a field if the area that needed to be covered consisted of 70,000 square feet?

Area and Perimeter of Rectangles *(Cont'd.)*

4. Based on the playing facilities listed below, make two statements comparing their sizes. For example, you may predict that a dugout is 20 times smaller than a basketball court or that a soccer field is 350% larger than a basketball court. Then find the actual area, and see how close your predictions were. Finally, find the perimeter of each facility.

Statement 1:

Statement 2:

Playing Facility	Dimensions	Area	Perimeter
Dugout	45 ft. by 5 ft.		
Soccer field	45 m. by 65 m.		
Basketball court	65 ft. by 35 ft.		
Locker room	80 ft. by 32 ft.		

Name _____

Golden Rectangles

1. A Golden Rectangle is a rectangle in which the ratio of its length to its width is about 1.6:1. Fill in the chart below.

	Dimensions	Ratio of Length to Width	Difference from Golden Rectangle Ratio
Locker room	60 ft. by 25 ft.		
Dugout	40 ft. by 5 ft.		
Basketball court	68 ft. by 42 ft.		
Soccer field	60 m. by 35 m.		

2. Which areas in the table in problem 1 have a ratio that approximates that of a Golden Rectangle?

3. Measure the length and width of various objects to find examples of Golden Rectangles. Some suggestions: flags, calculators, books, blackboards, windows, doors, file cabinets.

4. Predict the ratio of your height to the span of your two arms. Find the ratio. What did you learn?

Measurement and geometry

Name _____

Functions

In the exercises below, (1) write the function rule, and (2) solve for the variable. Then graph the functions on graph paper.

1. X = number of total shots by a team; Y = points earned.

   Function rule: _____

X	Y
8	1
11	$1\frac{3}{8}$
13	$1\frac{5}{8}$
10	n

2. X = number of fouls committed by a team; Y = points earned.

   Function rule: _____

X	Y
14	$-\frac{7}{12}$
16	$-\frac{2}{3}$
22	$-\frac{11}{12}$
25	n

Measurement and geometry

Functions *(Cont'd.)*

3. X = number of corner kicks by a team; Y = number of points earned.

   Function rule: _____

X	Y
3	$\frac{1}{3}$
7	$\frac{7}{9}$
10	$1\frac{1}{9}$
11	n

4. Construct your own function chart below.

   Function rule: _____

X	Y

Measurement and geometry

Name _____

Area and Circumference of Circles

Area of circle = πr^2

Circumference of circle = πd

r = radius; d = diameter; π = 3.14

1. A circular logo located at the center of the soccer field has a diameter of 30 feet. Find the area and circumference of the logo.

2. If the area of a circular logo is 706.5 square feet, what is the diameter of the circle?

3. On an elementary school soccer field, the circle surrounding the center mark has a diameter of 10 feet. What is the area of the circle?

4. A circular soccer stadium has a radius of 500 feet. Find the diameter, circumference, and area of the stadium.

   Diameter: _____

   Circumference: _____

   Area: _____

5. If the circumference of a logo on a shirt is 5.5 inches, what are the radius, diameter, and area of the logo?

   Radius: _____

   Diameter: _____

   Area: _____

Measurement and geometry

PRACTICE WORKSHEET 38

Weight

Predict and then find the weight of the following objects in the specified units. You will need a scale.

	Predicted Weight			Actual Weight		
	Pounds	Ounces	Grams	Pounds	Ounces	Grams
Soccer ball						
Basketball						
Tennis ball						
Hockey puck						

For each of the following problems, predict the answer, then solve the problem.

1. How many soccer balls would it take to weigh as much as 10 hockey pucks? As much as 1,000 tennis balls?

2. Which is greater: the weight of 20 footballs or 15 soccer balls?

3. How many soccer balls would it take to equal your body weight? How many tennis balls?

Measurement and geometry

Pythagorean Theorem

In a right triangle,

$$a^2 + b^2 = c^2$$

where

a = length of one leg of the triangle
b = length of the other leg of the triangle
c = length of the hypotenuse

Use the Pythagorean Theorem to solve the following problems.

1. Find the length of the diagonal of a soccer goal if the length of the goal is 7.32 meters and the width is 2.44 meters.

2. Find the length of the diagonal of a soccer field if the length of the field is 360 feet and the width is 225 feet.

3. Find the length of the diagonal of a soccer team's clubhouse if the length is 86 feet and the width is 30 feet.

4. Find the width of the goal area if the length is 40.23 meters and the length of the diagonal is 43.47 meters.

5. Find the length of half of a soccer field if the width of the field is 70 meters and the length of the diagonal for the field is 134.63 meters.

Measurement and geometry

Mean, Median, Mode, and Range

(Use with Handout 12)

1. For each of the first six weeks, find the points earned by each player on the Panthers. In the table below, record the mean, median, mode, and range for the points earned for each of the first six weeks.

Week	Mean	Median	Mode	Range
1				
2				
3				
4				
5				
6				

2. For each of the first six weeks, find the points earned by each player on your starting team. In the table below, record the mean, median, mode, and range for the points earned for each of the first six weeks.

Week	Mean	Median	Mode	Range
1				
2				
3				
4				
5				
6				

Statistics, data analysis, and probability

Name _____

Probability

1. Wen Lin kicked 30% of his goals from the left side of the field, 10% from the right side, and 60% from straightaway. If Lin had 30 goals this year, how many goals did he kick from each direction?

2. Using only the data in problem 1, what is the probability that Lin's next goal will be from the left side of the field?

3. A team's win-loss record during the past 10 years is 170–140. Without taking any other variables into account, what should the team's record be this year?

4. In how many ways can you express the outcome if the probability of an event occurring is 20%? *Hint: .20*

5. If the probability that an event will occur is .83, what is the probability that the event will not occur?

Statistics, data analysis, and probability

Probability *(Cont'd.)*

6. The letters in "Aiko Kobayashi" are placed into a hat. Find the probability of the following random events.

   A. Selecting the letter *k*

   B. Selecting the letters *a, y,* or *s*

   C. Selecting the letter *j*

   D. Selecting any letter except *a*

   E. Selecting the letter *h,* replacing it, then selecting the letter *h* again

   F. Selecting the letters *b* and *y* on consecutive draws (without replacing letters)

In exercises 7–11, you are given $P(Q)$, the probability that a player will successfully convert a penalty kick. Find $P(\text{not } Q)$, the probability that event Q will not occur.

7. $P(Q) = \dfrac{7}{12}$ $P(\text{not } Q) =$

8. $P(Q) = .85$ $P(\text{not } Q) =$

9. $P(Q) = 77\%$ $P(\text{not } Q) =$

10. $P(Q) = 1$ $P(\text{not } Q) =$

11. $P(Q) = 0$ $P(\text{not } Q) =$

Statistics, data analysis, and probability

Name _____

PRACTICE WORKSHEET 42

Circle Graphs

(Use with Handout 12)

$W \div S \times 360 = A$

W = total weekly points for one player
S = total weekly points for the team
A = the measurement of the central angle of the circle graph

Example

Jorge Sadon earned $1\frac{1}{8}$ points for week 1. Find the measurement of the central angle in a circle graph representing Sadon's portion of his team's total points for that week.

$$1\frac{1}{8} \div 8\frac{5}{24} \times 360 = 49°$$

1. Find the measurement of the central angles for Pedro Garcia, Yi Chen, and Lars Visser for week 5.

2. Find the measurement of the central angles for Pedro Garcia, Yi Chen, and Lars Visser for week 3.

3. Find the measurement of the central angles for the cumulative points for the Panthers for weeks 1–6.

4. If the central angle in a circle graph is 45 degrees, what percentage of the graph will that section represent?

5. If the central angle in a circle graph is 172 degrees, what percentage of the graph will that section represent?

6. If one section of a circle graph represented 38% of the total graph, what is the measurement of the corresponding central angle?

PRACTICE WORKSHEET 43

Stem-and-Leaf Plots and Histograms

1. The following values represent the point totals (in 24ths) for the Panthers for the first 10 weeks of the season. Using graph paper, construct a stem-and-leaf plot and histogram. *Hint:* On the stem-and-leaf plot, let the tens digits form the stems and the ones digits form the leaves.

155   183   177   194   189
152   185   177   163   159

2. The following values represent the point totals (in 24ths) for Hiroshi Nakamura for the first 10 weeks of the season. Using graph paper, construct a stem-and-leaf plot and histogram based on the data below.

11   12   10   18   15
28   14   7   16   32

Statistics, data analysis, and probability

Name _____

Scatter Plots

1. The table below represents a player's age and number of goals scored over the course of several seasons. On graph paper, construct a scatter plot of these data. Does the scatter plot have a positive or negative correlation? Explain your answer.

Age	Number of Goals
20	27
21	28
22	19
23	15
24	16
25	14
26	9
27	12
28	6
29	4

2. The table below shows the average number of minutes played per game and the number of yellow cards for several players for one season. Using graph paper, construct a scatter plot for these data. Does the scatter plot have a positive or negative correlation? Explain your answer.

Player	Average Minutes Played	Number of Yellow Cards
A	87	27
B	51	17
C	33	8
D	77	18
E	83	31
F	23	5
G	59	19
H	86	29
I	78	20

Statistics, data analysis, and probability

139

PRACTICE WORKSHEET 45

Box-and-Whisker Plots

The following data sets represent the points earned (in 24ths) by Paul Belair and the total team points earned by the Panthers for the final 12 weeks of the season. Using graph paper, draw a box-and-whisker plot for each set of data. Label the medians as well as the upper and lower quartiles.

1. Paul Belair   33, 4, 27, 13, 22, 10, 0, 19, 17, 4, 25, 29

2. Panthers   144, 181, 166, 150, 206, 177, 273, 111, 249, 243, 195, 199

Statistics, data analysis, and probability

Name _____

Statements Using Math Terminology

(Use with Handout 12)

Statements are complete sentences based on a set of data, and they must be accompanied by mathematical proof. The following statements were derived from Handout 12.

Example

Lars Visser earned half as many points for week 5 as he earned for week 4.

$$\frac{1}{2} \times 1\frac{1}{3} = \frac{2}{3}$$

For the following statements, show the mathematical proof.

1. Yi Chen earned more cumulative points than Lars Visser.

2. Lars Visser accounted for approximately 25% of the total points earned in week 1.

3. Pedro Garcia earned approximately 26% of the Panthers' total points in week 4.

4. The difference between Lars Visser's and Yi Chen's cumulative points for weeks 1–6 is $\frac{5}{8}$.

5. Use Handout 12 to write five statements, and show the mathematical proof for each.

　1.

　2.

　3.

　4.

　5.

Mathematical reasoning   141

Extra Credit Problems

1. A soccer ball is dropped from the top of the Eiffel Tower in Paris, which has a height of 986 feet. Each time the ball bounces, it rebounds to 38% of its height on the previous rebound. Construct a table of the number of bounces and the rebound height of each bounce. On which bounce does the ball bounce less than 1 foot high?

2. Find the stadium seating capacity, average ticket price, and revenue for your favorite soccer team. In this case, revenue is defined as the number of tickets sold, multiplied by the average price of a ticket, multiplied by the number of regular season home games the team plays during one season.

   A. How much would revenue increase for one game for your favorite team if ticket prices increased by an average of 5%?

   B. How much would revenue decrease for the season if your team decreased ticket prices by an average of 3%?

3. Create a new scoring system using fractions, decimals, exponents, factorials, roots, integers, or summations. Then compute your weekly points in that scoring system.

4. Predict how many small (8-inch diameter), medium (12-inch diameter), or large (16-inch diameter) pizzas would fit on a soccer field. Then find the actual number of pizzas.

Assessment

Name _____

Pretest/Posttest

Show all of your work.

1. Find the sum of the points earned by the following players:

   Ting Wan $1\frac{5}{24}$ Iva Hayashi $\frac{17}{24}$

   Ramon Ortiz $\frac{5}{6}$ Olivia Stemme $1\frac{1}{8}$

   Ronaldo Rivera $\frac{3}{8}$ Darcy Camus $1\frac{1}{6}$

   Joscelin Breitenbach $\frac{2}{3}$ Xue Yuan $\frac{5}{12}$

2. In problem 1, what is the ratio of the points earned by Darcy Camus compared to the points earned by Iva Hayashi?

3. In problem 1, convert Ting Wan's points into a decimal, and round to the nearest thousandth.

4. Evaluate

$$\frac{1}{4}(G) + \frac{1}{6}(S + A) - \frac{1}{12}(Y + R) + \frac{1}{8}(T) - \frac{1}{24}(F + O)$$

   when

   $G = 2$
   $S = 1$
   $A = 2$
   $Y = 1$
   $R = 0$
   $T = 14$
   $F = 19$
   $O = 3$

Pretest/Posttest *(Cont'd.)*

5. If one factor of $\frac{18}{24}$ is $\frac{3}{4}$, what is the second factor?

6. Write the prime factorization of 135 using exponential notation.

7. Convert $\frac{43}{24}$ into a mixed number, and write it in the simplest form.

8. Which is the higher average per game: 64 saves in 11 games or 77 saves in 13 games?

9. If Huan Xia accumulated 7.25 points during the first third of the season, how many points is he projected to earn for the entire season?

Pretest/Posttest *(Cont'd.)*

10. Based on the data in problem 1, find the following:

    Range

    Mean

    Median

    Mode

11. Fill in the missing numbers in the patterns below:

    Feliciano Santos $\dfrac{3}{8}$ $\dfrac{3}{4}$ _____

    Enrique Sanchez $\dfrac{5}{12}$ $\dfrac{5}{6}$ $1\dfrac{1}{4}$ _____

12. The price of a jersey autographed by Helena Ferreira rose from \$125 to \$235. Find the percentage of the price increase.

13. If a player invests 15% of his annual salary of \$15 million at 7.5%, how much interest will he earn after one year?

14. The dimensions of the parking lot at a soccer stadium are 850 feet by 1,550 feet. Find the area of the parking lot in square inches.

15. In problem 14, what is the length in feet of the diagonal of the parking lot?

Pretest/Posttest *(Cont'd.)*

16. The letters in "Gabriella Gustafsson" are placed into a hat. Find the probability of the following random events:

    A. P (selecting the letter a)

    B. P (selecting the letters p, i, or l)

17. Solve for the variable.

$$\frac{1}{4}(2) + \frac{1}{6}(1 + 0) - \frac{1}{12}(1 + 1) + \frac{1}{8}(T) - \frac{1}{24}(12 + 4) = 1$$

Assessment

William McMiller MD
Dr. Bill's Learning Centers
18 Lake St. Oak Park
4909 W. Division Chicago
708-434-0336